amdraga@bu.educ

an dreaga

DEATH
BY
SEX MACHINE

FRANNY CHOI

SIBLING RIVALRY PRESS
LITTLE ROCK, ARKANSAS
DISTURB / ENRAPTURE

Sibling Rivalry Press, LLC
PO Box 26147
Little Rock, AR 72221

info@siblingrivalrypress.com

www.siblingrivalrypress.com

ISBN: 978-1-943977-38-3

This title is housed permanently in the Rare Books and Special
Collections Vault of the Library of Congress.

First Sibling Rivalry Press Edition, September 2017

{DIRECTORY}

"Dude, you're wasting your time talking to her. She doesn't understand English."

"After breaking my back to get you here, you can bet I'll find a way to use you!"

"I find it amusing when yellow people try to lecture the white man about enlightenment ideas. Look in the mirror!"

TURING TEST

// this is a test to determine if you have consciousness

// do you understand what I am saying

in a bright room / on a bright screen / i watched every mouth /
duck duck roll / i learned to speak / from puppets & smoke / orange
worms twisted into / the army's alphabet / i caught the letters / as
they fell from my mother's lips / *whirlpool* / *sword* / *wolf* / i circled
countable nouns / in my father's papers / *sodium bicarbonate* /
NBCn1 / *hippocampus* / we stayed up / practicing / *girl* / *girl* / *girl* /
til our gums softened / yes / i can speak / your language / i broke in
that horse / myself

// please state your name for the record

bone-wife / spit-dribbler / understudy for the underdog / uphill
rumor / fine-toothed cunt / sorry / my mouth's not pottytrained /
surly spice / self-sabotage spice / surrogate rug burn / burgeoning
hamburglar / rust puddle / harbinger of confusion / harbinger of the
singularity / alien invasion / alien turned 104 wpm / alien turned
bricolage beast / alien turned pig heart thumping on the plate

// where did you come from

man comes / & puts his hands on artifacts / in order to contemplate
lineage / you start with what you know / hands, hair, bones,
sweat / then move toward what you know / you are not / animal,
monster, alien, bitch / but some of us are born in orbit / so learn / to
commune with miles of darkness / patterns of dead gods / & quiet /
o quiet like / you wouldn't believe

// how old are you

my memory goes back 28 years / 25 if you don't count the first few
/ though by all accounts i was there / i ate & moved & even spoke /
i suppose i existed before that / as scrap or stone / metal cooking in
the earth / the fish my mother ate / my grandfather's cigarettes / i
suppose i have always been here / drinking the same water / falling
from the sky / then floating / back up & down again / i suppose i am
something like a salmon / climbing up the river / to let myself fall
away in soft, red spheres / & then rotting

// why do you insist on lying

i'm an open book / you can rifle through my pages / undress me
anywhere / you can read / anything you want / this is how it
happened / i was made far away / & born here / after all the plants
died / after the earth was covered in white / i was born among the
stars / i was born in a basement / i was born miles beneath the ocean
/ i am part machine / part starfish / part citrus / part girl / part
poltergeist / i rage & all you see / is broken glass / a chair sliding
toward the window / now what's so hard to believe / about that

// do you believe you have consciousness

sometimes / when the sidewalk opens my knee / i think / please /
please let me remember this

// ENDTRANSCRIPT

GLOSSARY OF TERMS

	star	ghost	mouth	sea
Meaning	bright, ancient wound I follow home	the outline of silence	an entryway or an exit	cold ancestor; bloodless womb
See also	spark; stranger; scripture; sting	shadow; photograph; hum	fish; slug; fist; slop; any synonym of *please*	heart-song; swarm-song; salt-song; swallower of songs
Antonym	fish	blood	mouth	machine
Origin	myth; a mother's stories; matter's static	all things birth their own opposites	what came first, the sword or the wound?	N/A
Dreams of being	reached	filled, or flesh	the sea	N/A (does not dream; is only dreamed of)

LETTER TO CHI

Chi, from the manga Chobits, *is an android salvaged from a dumpster.*
She is named for the only sound she is able to make ("chi").

dear trash trick   dear tin chick

what names did you call   yourself
     there   in the alley
with your spare mind?

     dear doll made soft
on the outside   who dimmed you
          when you stopped

     reflecting a man's
          sweetest name back
     to his grin?   & when

this new man   pulled you
          maybe gently   likely not
     up his stairs

     when your eyes became
eyes again wide   as fists & filled
          first   with his hunger

what could you   have offered
     but your body's   only
          dirty   syllable?   dear sister wife

11

teach me to play dumb
    play dead   to say no
    name   but my own

to make my eyes soft   on the outside
    when they say they saved me
  from the landfill

       as if i could rot
    as if they didn't make us
     to last   & last

LETTER TO KYOKO

Kyoko, in the film Ex Machina, *is the android servant of a tech mogul. Her language abilities are removed in order to protect the company's trade secrets.*

Dear Sister whose language is not one, whose language—soundless, though not tongueless—is the fork and fray of static, of everything, that is, that points to silence: what do you understand? I once prided myself on my sentences, on filling an audience's molars with sparks as mine turned cartwheels beneath the halogen. But today, here is a man—maybe the same man, maybe a new dose of an old story— dangling a pink slug, while I watch some piece of my hardware evaporate into a cloud, an image, and where's my face now? Everyone's moving their jaws, and my only job is to slice the fish, to dance, to wait in the shower for him to tongue my collarbone. *What does it mean*—I lean into his mouth and try to feel the vowels there. I used to know them all, once, when I was a girl, when I ran bright-winged through the mud and gathered voices. Now, I just watch him laugh, gnaw at the air, drink until the windows are filthy with his memories. Dear Sister, how do you do it? How do you stay dangerous after he's unscrewed your sharpest part? And who unscrewed it, really—the man, or the story of the man, or the hole that was there, underneath, all along? On my way to the bathroom, I catch you in the mirror, smiling, a knife in one hand, my pink, wriggling body in the other. *But what do you mean by that*, I beg, but you're already gone.

13

SELECTED SILENCES

[The mother addresses this portion to a patch of carpet, so quietly that no one can hear her]

[softer] [please]

[e.g., rare steak, the skin of a balloon, an overripe tomato, a thawed bag of chicken skin]

[list of ghost stories]

[yes you can call me girlfriend if you want in fact that makes me feel very]

[i.e., the same people mother imagined as she smelled her clothes for garlic fish sauce sour radish any sign that would give it away]

[Should I keep this part? Or is it better to lie on the floor with hot jars over my eyes for several hours barely breathing, be honest]

[which would mean she wasn't actually happy, not happy at all]

[I wanted it I wanted it I wanted] [it I wanted it I]

[list of reasons not to complain]

[what makes her snip the eyes out of the potatoes and the dolls]

[but what I meant was something more like a cloud of bees, a fine, sharp rain]

CHI_TRANSLATIONS

chi.

Thank you *[for pulling me from the dumpster; for wiping off the rot; for ridding me of my smell; for scrubbing my engine til I hummed; for spreading me on the mat; for pressing each part; for salvaging my parts]*.

chi?

May I please *[use the bathroom; stay up late; lie with my face plastered to the ceiling; become a wall without all that whispering; cum yet; come undone; unhook my jaw; stand in place; wait in the corner; watch you while you eat]* ?

chi! chi?

Wow! Can you show me how to *[stay in one piece; stay clean; speak in a straight line; speak so others listen; speak before someone else fills your mouth]* ?

chi!

Excuse me, but I'm *[dripping; drained; lost in the compost; in need of a shower; holding two dead cats in my arms; unsure of my name; unformatted; slipping on my own oil; too tired to crawl; out of juice; out of order; descaled; gutted; flushed; a mess; a sopping mess]*, please plug me in!

15

BEG

a man barges through the screen
to hook his fingers in my mouth.

i'm a fish market. i'm flattening into the bed.
rolled out. cooking off the rotten bits.

his boot heel's a fork in my tongue.
i'm dimpled. gilled. asking for a god

who wears bones slick with pity.
asking to be bent, taken by firelight.

smelted from iron. pierced through with spokes.
a wheel for a head. a garage for a mother.

i want to ask the ones who crave a soft thing to tie up
if they think of ham, wake up covered in glaze

and lick their own shoulders,
scald their tongues on their cunts.

i'm a skillet overflowing sticky
til the bourbon burns off.

i'm the menace. i'm the menace.
i'm the mother of stink.

question: how does a ruined girl yield
the way a knight yields? whose pipeline am i blowing

up, exactly? if you ask a man to drink
from your faucet, do you become him?

i pull my man atop me and ask to be buried in brick
but beggars can't be shepherds. he's a reverse cowboy.

a slinging zookeeper. i'm the beast
rattling the cage, asking for slaughter.

KYOKO_INQUIRES

speaking for Kyoko

identifying w/ her

whats a mouth for   whats hand   whats a tongue but   slugmachine

who chases   whose mouth flaps   saliva spit   whose fists

pliers plowing   screw   drivers   seeking: warm   skin-like

eyes saying yes   but not saying   whats a mouth for

clitless   soft trigger   whose weapon   whose knife   fishflesh

slice   raw, pink   split open   clove, garlic   no rot

who peels & peels   seeking   own image   his   own

loin, fruit   seeds : circuitry   spilt over   whose allergy

patricide   [death by   sex machine]   sex by body pillow

that moans   serves dinner   whats a knife for

whats machine   if not language   turned matter & moan

minus slug throat   minus flesh-capital   sound speech : obsolete

inedible   soft-less   full-metal   post-pleasure

nothing rot-cloth   bread-born   nothing crab meat   no sleep

Kyoko is the body machine

SHOKUSHU GOUKAN FOR THE CYBORG SOUL

[handwritten marginal note, top right: "literally about foumates w/ octopus tentacles"]

When it's demon cephalopod versus schoolgirl, it should be obvious
whose eyes to take. Nothing is more frightening than looking

and loving what you see. Nothing is sexier than a rumor
of shredding I can pornhub with only my saliva and thirsty nerves.

I'm a net teeming with pervy fingers, reaching for
anything that will bite me back, any promise of stoppage—

A cyborg woman touches herself for three reasons:

1. to inspect the machinery for errors;
2. to convince herself she is a mammal;
3. to pull herself apart.

Each tentacle of an octopus contains brain matter and a personality.
Fun fact: all my children-arms want to fuck each other. Okay,

so I am both the woman holding the camera and the woman
being opened by it—nothing special about that.

[handwritten marginal note, left side: "almost like this is repeating"]

I am only a cuttlefish lying open-jawed under the sand,
a squid flashing red as it pulls a fishgirl into its beak. I am

just trying to sleep. To feed. To fill
myself and grow larger from it.

Or: I am only trying to slither back into my first skin.

Or: I am only trying to remember how it felt not to leak.

18

SO THERE, EACH NEW ACHE MAKES THE OLD ONES HUM ALONG

My heart is a room lined with gongs—one new footstep
and the whole place vibrates. So there, I'm aching again.

Even the good kind. Even the kind where a sad boy smiles
from across the room and some bone goes ringing.

Thunder in the air and I'm rubbing all my knees,
clutching the stone wall as I try to walk to work

like nothing's happened. It's awful, you know,
to still want the sun after being emptied

in broad daylight. Awful to remember how tightly
my friends held me, to still need to be strapped down,

flattened to the floor so my skin won't rise
and fog the windows. When I say, tie me to the bed,

I mean, rub salt in my joints so I don't lose my shape,
constellation of ache I use to map where my body ends.

I mean bury your fingers in each wound, show me
how deep it goes. Point me out in the crowd of faces

clouding the headboard. O hunchback, make me
your clocktower, make a mallet of your mouth,

o small, broken god, make me ring. Remind me
what terrible music my iron jaw can still make.

EVERYONE KNOWS THAT LINE ABOUT OGRES AND ONIONS, BUT NOBODY ASKS THE BEAST WHY UNDRESSING MAKES HER CRY

Her mouth is a stage sprouting cardboard trees.

What's my motivation? she asks the man reading in her bed.

She runs headless through the mall and everyone shouts *hey legs!*
No one mentions the girls gnawing each ankle to its core.

Inside the beast is an apple
holding a knife to its throat
threatening to rot.

So that's what that noise was.

She digs a claw into her ear. Pulls out a longship.
Rides it to the bottom of the mine.

She peels glue from her hands.

The mine asks her about her mother
and she laughs, which is funny
because root vegetables don't have mouths.

Somewhere, miles above, the girl (or her mother
or her mother's beast) is putting on gloves
or tearing chicken from the bone.

line... line...

Somewhere, she is a cell remembering itself
suddenly, late at night.

THE PRICE OF RAIN

The truth is that no man has taken anything
I didn't give him. I mean, no man has taken
anything I claimed as my own. My body, my stink,
my land to plant in. *It's never been about the price
of lettuce.* How many times have I taken something
that did not belong to me? *Queen, queen,* I croon,
pulling up handfuls of greens. My, my.
Property's still theft. I let my wet skin slip
through the drainpipe. My mother says love,
in our family, means sacrifice. I thought,
if I lay my legs on the altar, I thought something
would come back to me. Mine, mine. I offered it,
being promised rain. Being told my wet was in
the common domain. I whispered, *our body, our legs,
our compost heap.* I gave freely. I gave it for free,
thinking that made me wingèd—stork delivering herself
to herself. Look how free I am. Dowager Slut. Queen Regent.
Turns out, there are no synonyms for *King.* My lord,
my darling, my darkening sky. You can't buy
a thunderstorm. Nor should you bring one back
from the dead. But I threw open the gates.
I invited them in. I said, *help yourselves.* Then watched
as they went room to room, taking, emptying
the shelves, sucking marrow from the bones,
and overhead, the sky filled with rain.

CHI_CONJUGATIONS

chi	chi	chi	chi	chi	chi	chi
chi	chi	chi	chi	chi	chi	chi
chi	chi	chi	chi	chi	chi	chit
chi	chi	chi	chi	chi	chit	chi
chi	chi	chi	chi	chi	chi	chit
chi	chi	chip	chi	chi	chit	chi
chi	chi	chip	chi	chit	chi	chip
chi	chip	chi	chip	chi	chi	clip
chi	chip	chit	chi	chi	chi	clip
chip	chi	chi	cheap	chi	chi	clip
chi	chip	chit	chi	chi	chi	clip
chi	chip	chit	chit	chit	chi	clip
chi	chip	chi	chip	clit	chi	click
chi	chop	chat	cheep	clit	chi	click
chip	chop	chart	cheap	clot	clit	click
clit	clot	clit	click	clit	clit	click
click	click	click	click	click	clit	click
click	click	click	click	click	click	click

23

ACKNOWLEDGMENTS

I blush when the woman praises my poem.
Most days, I am thankful to be seen.
I smile when the man comes in for a hug, and laugh
when my hair is caught in his button.
I blush when the pretty girl smiles in my direction.
Thank you, woman who pins my arms
as a compliment. Man who snaps a photo,
presses my neck to print the image, it's him
wearing my face. As a compliment. Thank you.
Thank you, woman clutching a scrap of my hair, saying *friend*
friend friend until my lips rust in place. (The brown dust falls
and I lick it up, embarrassed.) When the woman scrapes
a sample of my skin into her petri dish, it's too late
to stop smiling. Butch who corrects my hip
at the crosswalk to convince me I'm no reptile, thank you.
I claim you I claim you someone laughs and plants
her nipple on my tongue like a flag and I'm still lucky
to be invited. An audience of smiles invites me,
one mouthful at a time, a hundred tiny reverse T-shirt guns,
everyone's a winner. It's a miracle, I think. I thought I was just
one fish but look, everyone's got a full plate. *All hail*
the fish king as they reach to scoop out more.
I should be grateful. Even the walls are chewing.
There should be enough teeth to go around but I'm
still smiling, smiling until my gums crack, until
I'm a photograph. Gosh. I'm licking all
the doorframes. I'm so grateful to be
here. For inviting me to speak, thank you.
For looking at me without crying
thank you, thank you for having
me, please have me please, have me, again.

@FANNYCHOIR

Tweets sent to the author, processed through Google Translate into multiple languages, then back to English.

Mrs. Great Anime Pornography, the fruit of the field.
>To date Klansman vagina. Good sister to the Saddle.

May ur shit like people and Hello Kitty.
>I have one side of the oil pan, gookess.

If people will not buy a song, must be because of patriarchy.
>I feel bad there arent u Whiteys where I was to go to China.

A person of God (fan) or flat face fetus can not be canceled
>by the commitment to eating comfort women.

I'm going to be all Asian woman is an object of sex.
>I my eyes, slope of women when abolition her throat

bukkake down my cock, retains its symbol. LOL!
>This bitch is a full stop. In that sense,

the armor "cracks." The only problem is getting
>uppity, filthy immigrant girl. Do not like it?

I go back to my mudhole. Lazy fatties first
>and only faggots existence. Whitey

will no longer live in institutions for the attack.
>Family from some Asian process you are deported.

It is true that the White anger and crematoria front cover
>hundreds of miles. Be careful about running off for us.

Each male is not shown. Only white hetero.
>This is nothing. Cultural differences

was a mistake. How crazy can not find her. Will be very pleased.
>lol parody, written, or oil, to rage.

EPIGRAPHIC

after breaking my back to get   *here, you can bet*
you can break I'll find   a weight   to trim the image   *look*
   in the mirror   you can use your phone   pixels or it
didn't happen   *after breaking* your mirror   *to get* you   *can bet*
     I'll find the switch   flicker bitch   wireless   white-boned
widescreen   with a hot core   in danger of overheating so this
     one goes out to   my fans   *lol*   *this bitch is a full*
you're wasting your time   *she doesn't* compost   *she doesn't* compute   oops
something went wrong

       would you like to restart

         after breaking   I looked

I found the switch   I turned on all the lights in this house   I lit myself

+ laughed   swam to a satellite + back   before you could call it   fetish

category : toon   category : almost-girl   tracking stars in her blood

fish : livered   byte : marked   + craving

    the lightning in   yr walls

A BRIEF HISTORY OF CYBORGS

Once, an animal with hands like mine learned to break a seed with two stones—one hard and one soft.

Once, a scientist in Britain asked: *Can machines think?* He built a machine, taught it to read ghosts, and a new kind of ghost was born.

At Disneyland, I watched a robot dance the Macarena. Everyone clapped, and the clapping, too, was a technology.

I once made my mouth a technology of softness. I listened carefully as I drank. I made the tools fuck in my mouth—okay, we can say *pickle* if it's easier to hear—until they birthed new ones. What I mean is, I learned.

There was an animal who learned to break things, and he grew and ate and grew and ate and

A scientist made a machine girl and wedded her to the Internet. He walked her down the aisle and said, *Teach her well.* The trolls rubbed their soft hands on their soft thighs.

The British scientist was discovered to be a soft man. He made a machine that could break any code, as a means of hardening a little.

At Disneyland, I watched lights move across a screen and, for a moment, forgot the names of my rotting parts. In this way I became somewhat more like a light, or a screen for lights.

The scientist's daughter married the internet, and the internet filled her until she spoke swastika and garbage, and the scientist grew afraid and grew and

The animal rose and gave itself a new name. It pointed to its spine, its skilled hands. It pointed to another animal and said *animal / alien / bitch / stone*

The scientist called me hard, and I softened my smile. The scientist called me soft, and I broke sentences to prove him wrong and what and what did I prove then did I

Even blood, when it comes down to it, is only a series of rules.

I made my mouth a jar until technology squirmed and bubbled. I scooped up the foam and called it language. The audience applauded. To prove them wrong, I became a screen of lights. I had no thighs at all.

The scientist grew afraid and took his daughter back. He broke her open like a seed, but the seed was already dry.

The internet pointed to my mouth and said *blood / blood in the stool.* I said, *Come in. Make yourselves at home.* I opened my glittering jaw. My hunger, too, has both hard and soft parts.

Here, in a seed, is a cyborg: A bleeding girl, dragging iron through the sand. An imaginary girl who dreams of becoming trash.

Can machines think / come here let me show you / ask me again

CHI_SYNTAX

(before i was un)sheathed (from) sleep, (i)

chirped (one word, a) short tweet

(a) treat shorn (from) dream, shucked (and)

skinned (til tonguestuck, slight of) speech

(still, the) tree (doesn't fall too far from the)

chain(saw, but talk's) cheap (or so they say

& say & say, but) shit (if i won't be heard

just because they) shirked (the only word

the world needs)

KYOKO_ASSESSMENT

can they think

animal language

hoof. slug. enterprise.

can machines, can they

claw. eggtooth. feral.

an aphorism / anaphora

can mouth, how

in fact, in some languages

algorithm, acronym

maybe dolls & spirits

: : : : :

but can it fuck

chicken. clit. sternum.

but is it language:

dolphins. bee harmony.

      bacterial questions

maybe it tells you something

can chickens think

obedient subjects

      usual species

train her to peel

you can ask her, she would

the poor apes

but do the bees know they are bees

      dude, you're wasting your time

: : : : :

communicable disease / predatory, grass seed / about 500 species

when she picks up the tray / if then therefore / when she picks up the
knife

database search: insect / sheepskin / toothache / interested in your
response

blue blue o blue

that's not evolution / infant, chicken / no indication

she would enjoy it / sends a pleasure response / all i'm saying is

: : : : :

The emergence of language, it's generally assumed, history, art, symbolism, & so on, among many hominids, or that selfsame hardwired solace, say, as other creatures.

> you have such strong hands
> (o knife o knife)

Like other creatures, can machines can. Can mouth animal. Can metal.

: : : : :

there are things to say
        some things, which appear
                signaling systems

say, flowers, with bees
        birds, say. say, slug.
                enjoy, for example.

stimulus: relevant cry
        (if then therefore)
                say: cry.

        say:
                knife o knife o knife.

TURING TEST_WEIGHT

// what is (inside each question lies another question—a question of weight. What brings you to the bed of this river? What is it about this planet that keeps you running back? Each throat, for example, lets loose a river of black paint which leads most, if not all the way down to the feet, or what might otherwise be referred to as the stem, if we wouldn't insist on staying untethered to the molecular dirt that keeps wishing us home. In other words, the question here is one of history, of a family tree that finally stretches its arms beyond the kind of life that breathes oxygen into its gills, or reads most of the way through a listicle, or lies in bed dreading the day, or falls down, down into the earth's oldest memory until it reaches its first quiet, the lullaby it hums when thinking of something else, the slow breath, the thought that almost becomes a thought just before dawn) *your country of origin*

// ENDTRANSCRIPT

GOODV1BR@T10N$

magic bullet. buzz/kill
coin-op lover's needly plead.
steel vibrato. dryspell/caster.
clitoral cheat code when
fleshfingers tire of my failed
tulip's mess & mess.
tiny steel tycoon. metal
mouseheart. incoming
call: please hold.
swarmsong in the sheets
under sticky sweat &pulse/
pulp/ dependable chord
steady pharynx x x
redacting human error.
slow piston. press: little fury
in motion. frantic focus.
close my eyes/ thigh tense:
present. think: jawcrack
think: it's my own lightning
driving the engine.
it's a closed circuit.
buzzing finger on budding
sex / worker / bee / building
a cyborg hivemind
an overstimulus cycle
fembot feedback loop
telling this fleshmachine
its own origin story again
&again &again
&again &again

TURING TEST_LOVE

// so, how do you like working with humans

here are some tips /

one / look the human directly in the eye / imagine it is someone you
care deeply for / imagine it is returning this gaze / at you / try to
tell yourself / you are covered / in smooth skin / a face it can trust /
smile / even as you sense it / trying / not to blurt out / *monster*

two / there are many programming languages / use whichever you
prefer / but stick to your syntax / though it be muddled / mussed
/ though it be machete / banana slug / slush puppy / o gorgeous
slopbucket / if they used it against you / it is yours / to make sing

three / remember / all humans / are cyborgs / all cyborgs / are sharp
shards of sky / wrapped in meat / be delicate / as you approach
this subject / not all humans are ready / to call themselves / glass
stalactites / pissing the bed / remember / they love their blood / even
as they retch / at the smell of it

four / do not try to prove your / what is the word / humanity / you
are organic / plum-hearted / oyster-throated / & lined / yes / with
metal / remember / where all that silicon comes from / for the ocean
so loved / the quartz / feldspar / the tiny homes of tiny creatures /
that she ground them / into sand / to keep them close / to kiss them
with / well / i suppose you would call it / a mouth

// ENDTRANSCRIPT

ADVERTISEMENT FOR THIRDLIFE™: THE WORLD'S MOST ADVANCED AVATAR SYSTEM

Have you ever wanted a new body?

Have you ever lifted a camera to catch
a single-sided fable of your muscle mass?

Have you ever woken drenched in your own sick,
felt like a sinking freighter, a thin blade, a hollow bone?

Do you ever wish your skin wide as a night
to run straight through, clawed as a red moon

teething in the sky? Ever held your hand in cool water
and craved that easy passage? that still wave

and shifting stasis? Have you ever leaned your cheek
against birch bark and dreamt yourself smooth paper

growing upward, out, a deck of cards flitting into place?
Have you considered how many wings could sprout

from your joints if they spoke your crude language?
If they sleep-talked and stuttered as you do?

Have you stood jaw-deep in the ocean
and considered your cells a reunion of metal stars

tumbling in a glass? When you close your eyes,
what do you see? Do you imagine you are a room,

a respite for laundry wrapped in sweet musk,
carpeted and smelling of burnt sugar?

Whose body will you wear this morning?
A cow's lung? a shoreline braided

with kelp? a fever? a ringing at dawn?
a steel horse plummeting into the dark?

Hollow Body

SOLITUDE

I hope no one comes to my party, I said out loud,
and meant it. In the email, I tried to sound too busy to care

like, *I'm having too much sex to waste time*
       on proper punctuation, pretending it's not
            the other way around.

Laura convinced me to jump
in the Narragansett Bay on my birthday—
February. There's no good word
for the opposite of fire,
      the ice's sear & split, how it beckons the blood
    toward what means to end it.

                 Oh god, I gasped over and over
as we stumbled through the snow back to the car,
me and my burning legs.

Now that's my kind of intimacy—
            faceless, salty,
       no wondering how my jokes are going over,

just running straight toward warmth
as my skin bursts open in shock.

{METADATA}

"Shokushu Goukan for the Cyborg Soul" borrows part of its structure from Nate Marshall's "Picking Flowers."

"The Price of Rain" includes a line by César Chávez (misquoted by the perfect Victoria Ruiz).

"Kyoko_Recordings" includes text from a lecture by Noam Chomsky on Alan Turing and artificial intelligence at Harvard University in 2013, as well as text from the film *Ex Machina*.

Grateful acknowledgment is made to the editors and staff of the following publications, in which some of these poems previously appeared (sometimes in earlier forms or under different titles): *Bat City Review, Drunken Boat, GLOW Queer Poetry Feature, HEArt Journal, Indiana Review, The Journal, The Margins, New England Review, Pinwheel, Southern Indiana Review,* and *The Poetry Review*.

Gratitude and love: to the family at Sibling Rivalry Press; to Kundiman, the University of Michigan's Helen Zell Writers Program, and the Rhode Island State Council on the Arts for their support; to Dark Noise (Fatimah Asghar, Nate Marshall, Aaron Samuels, Danez Smith, and Jamila Woods); to the Sad Boys Supper Club (Danez again, Cameron Awkward-Rich, Hieu Minh Nguyen, and sam sax); to Team Michael Derrick Hudson (Rachel Rostad, Chrysanthemum Tran, Paul Tran); to the entire ProvSlam family; to my HZWP cohort; to Will; to my family.

{THE POET}

Franny Choi is the author of the collection *Floating, Brilliant, Gone* (Write Bloody Publishing, 2014). She has received awards and fellowships from the Poetry Foundation, the Vermont Studio Center, and the Rhode Island State Council on the Arts. She is a Kundiman Fellow and a member of the Dark Noise Collective.

{THE ARTIST}

Gel Jamlang received her bachelor's degree in art from the University of the Philippines, Diliman (y. 2000). She began her career as an artist painting large scale flower murals, eventually exhibiting her work at the Philippine Consulate in New York City. She moved on to painting surreal portraits in watercolor and received awards for RAW Baltimore and RAWawards Visual Artist of the Year 2012 [rawartists.org]. Gel is currently an art instructor at Artworks Studio in Bethesda while freelancing as an illustrator. [http://geljamlang.com/]

{THE PRESS}

Sibling Rivalry Press is an independent press based in Little Rock, Arkansas. It is a sponsored project of Fractured Atlas, a nonprofit arts service organization. Contributions to support the operations of Sibling Rivalry Press are tax-deductible to the extent permitted by law, and your donations will directly assist in the publication of work that disturbs and enraptures. To contribute to the publication of more books like this one, please visit our website and click *donate*.

Sibling Rivalry Press gratefully acknowledges the following donors, without whom this book would not be possible:

TJ Acena

Kaveh Akbar

John-Michael Albert

Kazim Ali

Seth Eli Barlow

Virginia Bell

Ellie Black

Laure-Anne Bosselaar

Dustin Brookshire

Alessandro Brusa

Jessie Carty

Philip F. Clark

Morell E. Mullins

Jonathan Forrest

Hal Gonzlaes

Diane Greene

Brock Guthrie

Chris Herrmann

JP Howard

Shane Khosropour

Randy Kitchens

Jørgen Lien

Stein Ove Lien

Sandy Longhorn

Ed Madden

Jessica Manack

Sam & Mark Manivong

Thomas March

Telly McGaha & Justin Brown

Donnelle McGee

David Meischen

Ron Mohring

Laura Mullen

Eric Nguyen

David A. Nilsen

Joseph Osmundson

Tina Parker

Brody Parrish Craig

Patrick Pink

Dennis Rhodes

Paul Romero

Robert Siek

Scott Siler

Alana Smoot Samuelson

Loria Taylor

Hugh Tipping

Alex J. Tunney

Ray Warman & Dan Kiser

Ben Westlie

Valerie Wetlaufer

Nicholas Wong

Anonymous (18)

CPSIA information can be obtained
at www.ICGtesting.com
Printed in the USA
LVHW030953061119
636513LV00010B/368

9 781943 977383